The fantastically feminist
(and totally true) story of the
MATHEMATICIAN EXTRAORDINAIRE

ADA LOVELACE

ANNA DohERty

wren
& rook

Lord Byron is a superstar poet. He's very fashionable and loves to party! He leads a wild life and lots of people fall in love with him.

Lord Byron
1788–1824

Ada
1815–1852

AnNabella
1792–1860

MEET ADA's Family and Friends

ByroN
1836–1862

AnNe
1837–1917

Annabella loved to study when she was growing up, and she passes on her passion for maths and science to her daughter Ada. She can be quite strict at times, but she is brave for choosing to live as a single mum when it is very uncommon.

Mary is a brilliant Scottish mathematician and astronomer (that means she studies the stars and the night sky). She is Ada's maths tutor and friend. When she dies, one newspaper calls her the "queen of science".

Mary Somerville
1780–1872

William
1805–1893

Babbage is a very clever mathematician and inventor. In fact, he is so good at maths that he even works as a secret code-breaker for the government. He is one of Ada's very best friends.

Charles Babbage
1791–1871

Ralph
1839–1906

Mrs Puff

1816

THIS is LORD BYRON.

Lord Byron is Ada's dad. He is a poet and quite eccentric. He once had a pet bear and he likes to drink out of cups made from skulls. He is very clever but he can be pretty selfish, and is a rather nasty husband. You can only see his shadow here because at this very moment, his wife Anna-bella is moving out. She has had enough.

THIS is ANNABELLA and ADA.

Ada is a very young baby – she was only born five weeks ago. She and Annabella will go to live with Annabella's mum for a few years.

Annabella doesn't want Ada to grow up poetic and eccentric like her dad, so she asks the best tutors from all over the country to teach Ada 'non-imaginative' subjects like

MATHS, SCIENCE & LogIC.

Her teachers are very strict – Ada is punished if she doesn't work hard enough! Her favourite subjects are geography (she especially loves volcanoes) and maths.

1828

Ada loves steam engines and finding out how things work. She spends hours and hours designing her own flying machines, trying to build wings out of lots of different materials. She has just written a note to Annabella to explain her newest idea.

My dear MOTHER,

I am going to begin my PAPER WINgs tomorrow and I feel almost CONVINCED that with a year or so's experIEnce and practice I shall be able to bring the ART of FLYING to VERY GREAT PERFECTION. I think of writing A Book of FLYoLOGY...

YoUR VERY AFFECTIONATE CARRIER PIgEON

MRS PUFF

SHE HAS TO STAY IN BED FOR A WHOLE YEAR

Geometry

Arithmetic VOL. III

VOLCANOES

1829

Poor Ada is often ill as a girl. When she is 13 she gets terrible measles – she has to stay in bed for a whole year and hop about on crutches for ages afterwards!

She doesn't mind too much though, because it means she has plenty of time in bed to read and design new machines (and play with her best friend Mrs Puff).

MATHS etc.

STEAM ENGINES

FLYING

How trains Work

LORD BYRON'S POEMS

1832

Ada has lots of friends who are men, which isn't really allowed, and she likes to bet on horse races with them. This makes a lot of people think she is very scandalous. She even tries to run away to marry one of her tutors, but she gets caught.

Annabella is determined to make Ada behave more like a 'proper lady' and invites her friends round all the time to keep an eye on her daughter. Ada calls them The Furies because she says they make up stories about her to make her seem even more rebellious than she really is! (Perhaps so they can keep coming round for cups of tea.)

1833

Annabella has hired a tutor called Mary Somerville to teach Ada maths. The three women get along wonderfully, and Mary invites Annabella and Ada along to a party being hosted by an engineer named Charles Babbage. Lots of other famous people called Charles, like Charles Dickens and Charles Darwin, are likely to attend.

The three friends are on their way to the party right now. They are chatting about Ada's visit to the royal court three weeks earlier. Wealthy young women are 'presented' to the king when they are old enough to be married.

At the party, Ada meets Charles Babbage for the first time. Babbage is a bit of a science celebrity, famous for his gigantic and never-completed clockwork counting machines, which are like very early calculators. He is showing Ada his latest machine, called The Difference Engine.

No one else at the party can make head or tail of the machine, but Ada understands how it works immediately and is completely fascinated by it. From this moment on, Ada spends a lot of time with Babbage talking about their shared love of engines and maths (and also dogs and parrots). He tells her about his next counting machine, which will be called The Analytical Engine.

1835

Ada marries William King, Earl of Lovelace when she is 19. They have three children over the next four years.

MRS PUFF
BEST CAT EVER

WILLIAM

A nobleman and engineer. Wins an award for brick-making in 1851.

SCIENCE NEWS
LAST Night BABBAGE held Another of his FAMOUS PARTIES
more: PAGE 9

SCIENCE
BRICK MAKING

ANNE

Will eventually open a horse-breeding farm.

BYRON

Joins the navy when he grows up, and later becomes a shipyard worker.

HORSES
HORSE TALES
SHIPS & NAVY
MOUNTAINS
HORSE BREEDING
Maths.

1837

LORD · BYRON
POET · EXTRAORDINAIRE

While Ada was growing up, Annabella never let her see a painting of her dad in case she caught his 'madness'. But when Ada turns 20, Annabella decides she is old enough to look at his portrait.

(SOON-TO-BE) RALPH
- - - - - - - - - - - - -
Becomes an author and loves climbing in the Alps.

1842–3

Ada is hard at work translating a paper written by an Italian engineer called Luigi Menabrea.

It is about Babbage's Analytical Engine and Ada is adding in her own notes.

These notes will make her world-famous because she is thinking in ways that nobody ever has before. She has realised that the Engine …

"MIGHT ACT UPON OTHER THINGS BESIDES NUMBER … THE ENGINE MIGHT COMPOSE ELABORATE AND SCIENTIFIC PIECES OF MUSIC."

Babbage and other inventors have only ever talked about making machines that count (like calculators). It is Ada who first thinks that machines could be used for music, text, pictures and sounds. She is basically describing a computer!

THE ANALYTICAL ENGINE

1843

With all these new ideas, Ada helps Babbage update his design for the Analytical Engine. It is the very first design for a computer.

MeMORY

Although it is mechanical and run by steam, it still has a memory, which allows it to save numbers and answers to sums.

COGS

These work out the difference between numbers.

PRINTER

There's no screen, unlike today's computers and calculators. Instead, the machine prints out the answers for you!

PUNCH CARDS

Instead of buttons there are lots of 'punch cards' (cards with little holes in them to represent numbers) that you put into the machine. It uses them to work out calculations and sums for you.

1852

Sadly, Ada and Babbage don't manage to build The Analytical Engine.

Remember how Ada was sick a lot as a young girl? Unfortunately she starts to get sick a lot as an adult too.

Soon she is too ill to even leave the house, and Annabella moves in to look after her. Not many people come to visit because Annabella thinks Ada will get better faster if she is left alone. But Charles Dickens comes to read her his books and keep her company.

Sadly, Ada doesn't get better. And even though she hasn't seen her dad since she was a tiny baby, she asks to be buried next to him so they can be together for ever. Ada dies when she is just 36 years old.

1910–Today

In the end, Charles Babbage didn't manage to make the machine he and Ada designed. However, he did begin to build a smaller, simpler version of it, and in 1910, his son Henry Babbage completed what his father had started: The Analytical Engine Mill.

This was not the whole engine – it had no storage and couldn't do as many things as the one Ada and Babbage had designed.

But guess what? It works to this day and can print out the answers to sums. You can go and visit it at the Science Museum in London!

The Fantastically Feminist Ada Lovelace

To understand how amazing, daring and fantastically feminist Ada was, you have to know what it was like to be a woman when she was growing up. It was very different from today! Women and men were not given the same opportunities, and unfortunately people thought that women were less clever than men. This meant that girls often didn't get to go to school, and those who did were not taught scientific subjects – no chemistry, physics or maths.

However, Ada was lucky because her mum was fantastically feminist too. She encouraged her daughter to learn the same subjects that boys were taught, rather than what was expected of girls at the time.

Ada's father, Lord Byron, had been a poet (and not a very good husband), and Annabella didn't want her daughter to grow up like him. She encouraged Ada to follow her interest in maths, because it was scientific and very different from Lord Byron's pursuits. She managed to persuade some of the best mathematicians and scientists of the day to tutor Ada. It wouldn't have been easy to get university professors to agree to teach a little girl, but Annabella was determined that Ada should learn what she loved.

Annabella and Ada even travelled around the country visiting factories to see how machines worked in action. At this time, it was shocking that upper-class women could be interested in huge, dirty, noisy machinery! Women were expected to be interested in gentle activities, such as playing the piano and learning French. But Ada and Annabella didn't care what people thought, and refused to let society's rules stop them learning how engines worked.

Ada was strong-minded. She had been fortunate to receive the education she did, but that wasn't enough for her – she also wanted to keep learning even after she had grown up. But once girls finished schooling, they weren't allowed to go to university to study. If a woman wanted to continue her education, she had to find a teacher to give her lessons privately. So that's exactly what Ada did. She asked a university professor called Augustus De Morgan to teach her from home and she also started writing to famous mathematicians of the day, such as Charles Babbage and Luigi Menabrea. Ada was determined not only to learn all there was to know, but to discover even more for herself. Before long, she knew more than many of her teachers.

At that time, it was surprising for a woman to be interested in, and actually good at, maths. But Ada didn't hide her skills – she was very confident and would scribble corrections and additions on to scientific papers her mathematical friends wrote.

Ada's work with Babbage, together with the research she carried out on her own, allowed her to push mathematical machine inventions further than ever before. She was the first person to consider that 'counting machines' could do more than just count, which represented a huge leap forwards in technological understanding.

These ideas were so ahead of her time that it took nearly 100 years before they were actually recognised! Alan Turing, a Second World War codebreaker, used some of Ada's notes to help him work out how to build the first computer. And he wasn't the only person Ada influenced long after her death. For years, her work has helped to inspire countless women all over the world to take up careers in the sciences and maths.

Many scientific things are named after Ada, including a computer programming

language built by the US Department of Defence. And on the second Tuesday of October every year, Ada Lovelace Day is celebrated to honour Ada and all the amazing women who work in science, technology, engineering and maths.

Ada herself is remembered today because she found a way to learn about what she loved, even though society made it difficult for her. She knew what she wanted, and she went out and made it happen. She bravely found a way to pursue maths on her own and didn't let anything stand in her way. It was this daring, determined, feminist attitude that eventually established Ada as "the prophet of the computer age".

For Mum and Dad x

First published in Great Britain in 2019 by Wren & Rook

HB ISBN: 978 1 5263 6103 5
PB ISBN: 978 1 5263 6105 9
E-book ISBN: 978 1 5263 6104 2
10 9 8 7 6 5 4 3 2 1

MIX
Paper from
responsible sources
FSC® C104740
FSC www.fsc.org

Wren & Rook
An imprint of
Hachette Children's Group
Part of Hodder & Stoughton
Carmelite House
50 Victoria Embankment
London EC4Y 0DZ

An Hachette UK Company
www.hachette.co.uk
www.hachettechildrens.co.uk

Printed in China